The True Story of
BLOSSOM

The
Handicapped
OPOSSUM

**Story and Pictures by
NEAL WOOTEN**

ISBN 978-1-61225-467-8

Published by Mirror Publishing
Fort Payne, Alabama 35968

Printed in the USA.

Dedicated to all the little critters that call our woods home, and to all the people who selflessly care for them when needed.

Until one has loved an animal, a part of one's soul remains unawakened.
      - Anatole France

Hello. My name is Blossom. I'm an opossum. I live in the woods with my mom and brothers and sisters. I have ten total siblings. Yes... TEN! That's a lot.

We are North America's only marsupial. That means our mom has a pouch like a kangaroo. It sure got crowed with ten brothers and sisters. But now we're old enough to find food on our own. My brothers and sisters ran and played. How did they do that? My back legs don't move at all.

One day we were taking a ride on Mom. I couldn't hold on as well with only two hands, and I fell off. On no!

I knew she could not come back for me because that would put the others at risk. I was left all by myself. I wondered what creatures lurked here. Lions? Tigers? Bears? Yikes!

I dragged myself through the woods for hours. Then I heard a noise. Oh no, it was a giant monster human. He scooped me up in his mighty paw and took me to his home. I was

DOOMED.

He took me inside and placed me in a giant monster human chair. I hope he doesn't forget I'm here.

Hey, don't sit on me!

Another giant monster human came by and built a fenced area.

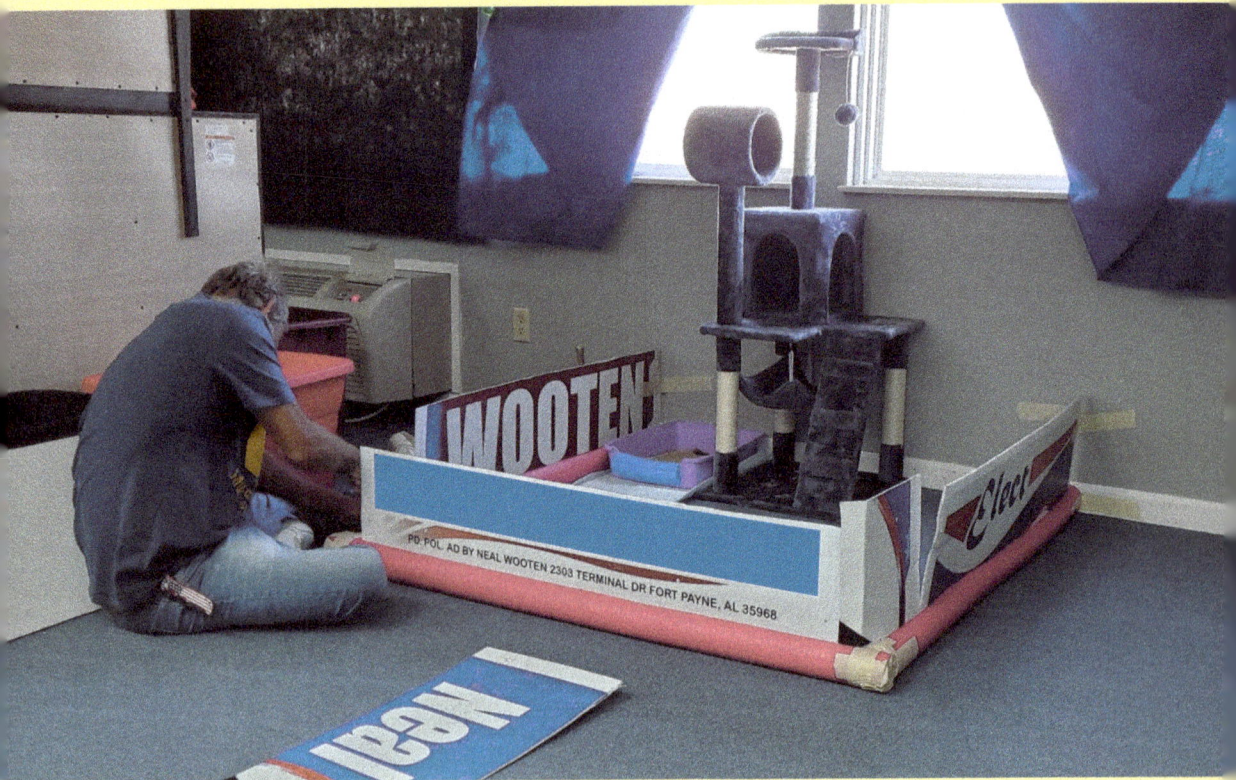

I could only wonder what mean, vicious, dangerous critter that was for.

Imagine my surprise when I found out it was for ME!

Delicate Instrument
Don't Drop

Every day that odd giant monster human would take me on the back deck and move my back legs

UP & DOWN

BACK & FORTH

$\mathcal{S}$ometimes I would grab his fingers with my back paws and try to push his hand away. But he'd just smile and say, "Good girl."

Some
days, if
there
was a
storm,
we'd
do our
exercises
on the inside. Sometimes I
could tell I had worked him
too hard.

I was eating well and getting stronger. I could even climb that cat tree thing.

Now that I was able to get around better, I thought it was time to pull my weight around here.

Okay, I found the problem. Your hearing aid is off.

No idle paws for me.

And I kept getting bigger and **bigger** and BIGGER.

Life was good, but I still longed to be with my own family in the woods. Then one day, the giant monster human took me into the woods...

AND...

Let me go. I found my mom and brothers and sisters and we were a family again.

I still go back at times since the human leaves food out every night. When he sees me, he still likes to rub my back. What's up with that?

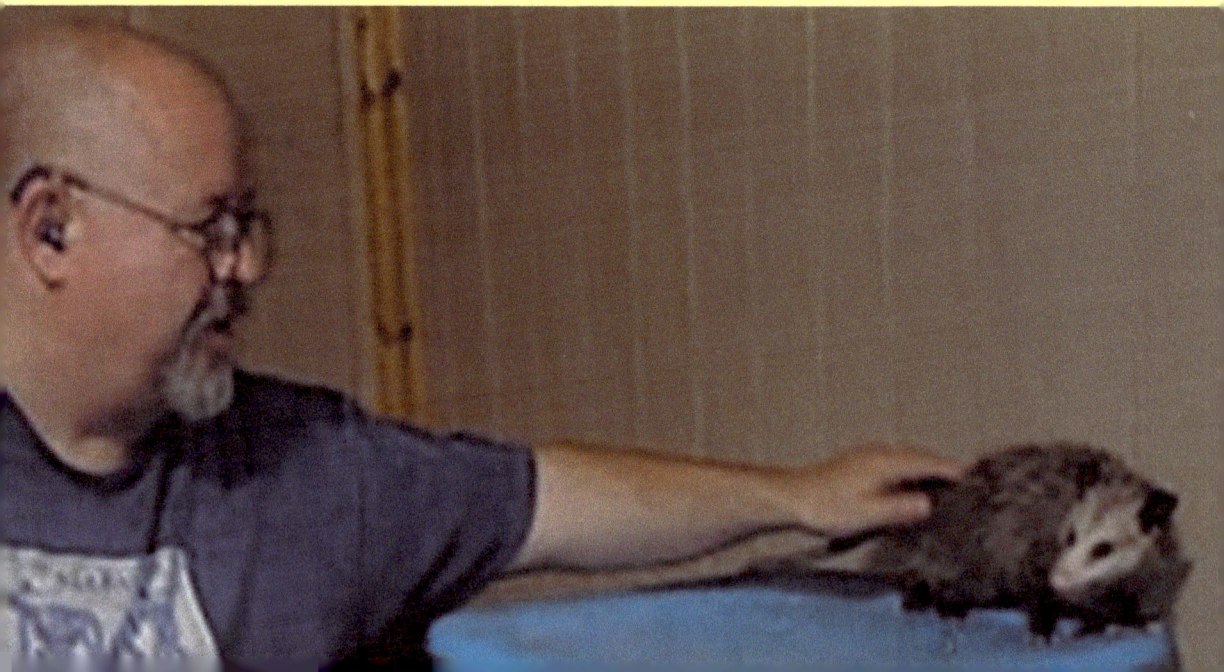

I have my own food dish.

Sometimes the silly cats think it's theirs.

Hey, you didn't leave any.

When my family goes with me, they always hide when the human comes around. Not me. I know I'm safe here.

*N*ow *I* know he's not a bad giant or a mean monster; he's just a big teddy bear.

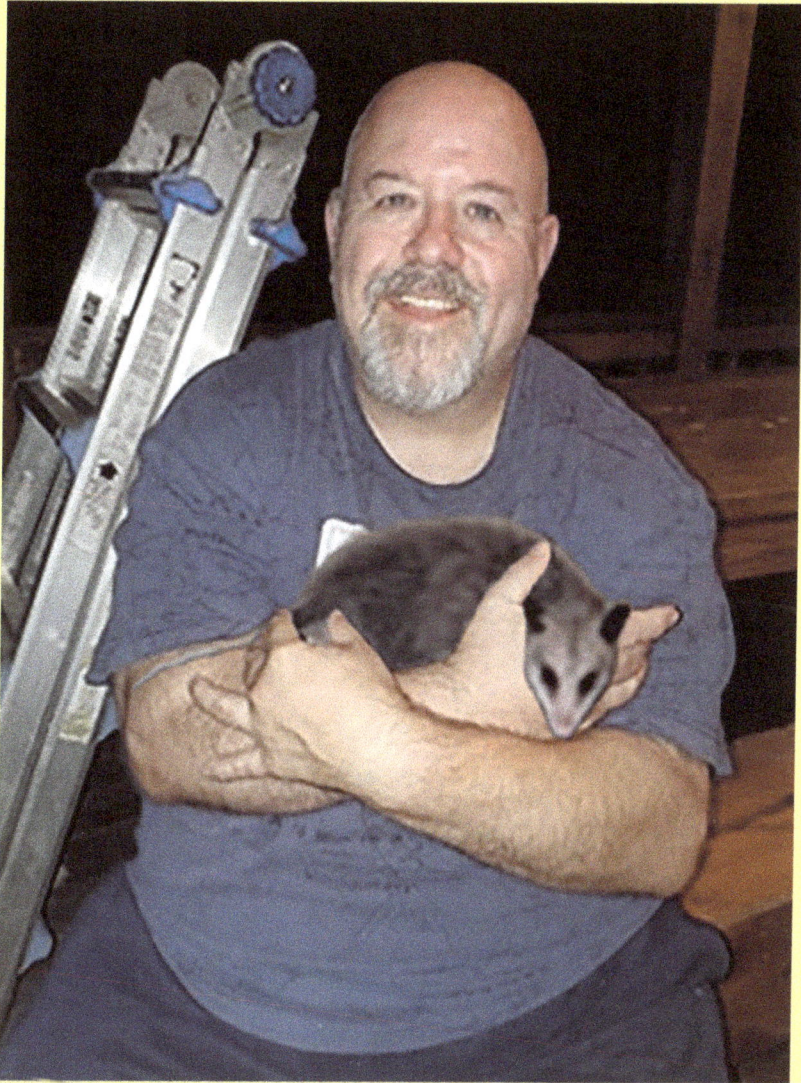

*A*re you an animal lover?

Ten Facts About Opossums

1. They're Not Aggressive
Even when confronted with a predator, they will use the infamous "playing possum" technique to appear dead and avoid an actual brawl. They can stay zoned out for hours, emitting a foul odor in order to further keep any bad guys at bay — but they'll never outright attack, even if they're baring their teeth.

2. They Rarely Have Rabies
Unlike most other wild animals, opossums are nearly completely immune to contracting rabies or passing it along.

3. They Kill Thousands of Ticks
According to stats reported by the National Wildlife Federation, a single opossum can potentially eliminate 4,000 ticks in one week thanks to their extreme self-grooming methods (either crushing or consuming the ticks burrowing in their fur).

4. They Won't Destroy Your Lawn or Property
Unlike other nocturnal animals creeping around neighborhoods, opossums won't destroy your lawn or property, and they don't spray like skunks.

5. They're True Survivors
They've been around longer than any other mammal. Opossums are often called "living fossils" because they've been able to survive on our planet for millions of years — over 70 million, to be exact, which really shows their ability to overcome adversity.

6. They Help with Waste Management

They are not picky eaters. If it's edible, they'll eat it —
including commonly dining on animals struck by vehicles on
the road (bones and all), which scientists refer to as "carrion."
This basically makes them nature's most efficient waste-
management team and cleanup crew.

7. They're the Only Marsupials Indigenous To North America

You have to admit, it would be a shame if Australia were the
only home to marsupials! Plus, it makes opossums even more
unique parts of our natural environment.

8. They Get Rid of Garden Pests

They aren't picky eaters when it comes to troublesome garden
pests like slugs, beetles, and cockroaches, but they will leave
the flowers or veggies you're growing undisturbed.

9. They May Be the Key To Battling Venomous Snake Bites

The venom of rattlesnakes, cottonmouths, and other
dangerous slithery snakes that might be hiding in your yard
has no effect on opossums.

10. They're Actually Quite Smart

Opossums tested with a higher intelligence than more
domestic animals like rabbits, dogs, and cats — particularly
when it came to finding good grub and remembering exactly
where it was to go back for more.